SONG OF THE SAY-SAYER

SONG OF THE SAY-SAYER

DANIEL DANIS

TRANSLATED BY
LINDA GABORIAU

TALONBOOKS

1999

Copyright © 1996 Daniel Danis
Translation © 1999 Linda Gaboriau

Talonbooks
#104—3100 Production Way,
Burnaby, British Columbia, Canada V5A 4R4

Typeset in New Baskerville and printed and bound in Canada by Hignell Printing Ltd.

First Printing: November 1999

Talonbooks are distributed in Canada by General Distribution Services, 325 Humber College Blvd., Toronto, Ontario, Canada M9W 7C3; Tel.:(416) 213-1919; Fax:(416) 213-1917.

Talonbooks are distributed in the U.S.A. by General Distribution Services Inc., 4500 Witmer Industrial Estates, Niagara Falls, New York, U.S.A. 14305-1386; Tel.:1-800-805-1083; Fax:1-800-481-6207.

 Canadä

The publisher gratefully acknowledges the financial support of the Canada Council for the Arts; the Government of Canada through the Book Publishing Industry Development Program; and the Province of British Columbia through the British Columbia Arts Council for our publishing activities.

An earlier version of *Le Chant du Dire-Dire* was published in the original French by Théâtre Ouvert, Paris, France, in 1996.

Canadian Cataloguing in Publication Data

Danis, Daniel, 1962-
    [Chant du Dire-Dire. English]
    Song of the Say-Sayer

    A play.
    Translation of: Le chant du Dire-Dire.
    ISBN 0-88922-419-6

    I. Title.
PS8557.A5667C5213 1999   C842'.54   C99-910801-8
PQ3919.2.D248C5213 1999

Le Chant du Dire-Dire was first produced in French by Espace Go and premiered in Montreal on April 28, 1998 with the following cast:

Pascal Contamine	FRED-GILLES
Kathleen Fortin	NOÉMA
François Papineau	ROCK
Stéphane Simard	WILLIAM

Directed by René Richard Cyr
Assisted by Allain Roy
Set design by Stéphane Roy
Costume design by Lyse Bédard
Lighting design by Guy Simard
Original Music by Michel Smith

The Song of the Say-Sayer was first produced in English, under the title *Thunderstruck or The Song of the Say-Sayer*, by One Yellow Rabbit and premiered in Calgary on February 23, 1999 with the following cast:

Denise Clarke	FRED-JAMES
Andy Curtis	WILLIAM
Michael Green	ROCK
Elizabeth Stepkowski	NAOMI

Directed by Blake Brooker
Staged by Denise Clarke
Assistant direction by Ken Cameron
Sound design by Richard McDowell
Set & Lighting design by Terry Middleton
Costume design by Tara Charran

This translation was made possible with the assistance of the 1997 Banff *playRites* Colony—a partnership between The Canada Council for the Arts, The Banff Centre for the Arts, and Alberta Theatre Projects.

This version of the translation incorporates revisions made by the playwright for the premiere production in France directed by Alain Françon at Théâtre de la Colline, Paris, September 1999.

Far from all eyes and ears, from any spoken word, far inside the body, deep in the silence of silence, one can secretly unite with one's soul-being and achieve an indifference to life and to death, allowing the body to fill with purity.

CHARACTERS

By age, their first names are ~~Rock, William, Fred-James~~, Naomi and they ~~are all named Lasting. All four were adopted and there might be three or four years difference between each of them.~~

Whether or not Naomi is visible on stage, depending upon the artistic vision of the director, it is essential that she be very alive, we should sense her breath; very physical, we should feel her humanity; very aware, we should feel she is a real presence.

THE SONG

At two or three moments in the performance, it would be appropriate to hear the three brothers produce throat music akin to the act of breathing, like certain types of African and Inuit chanting. Not a single recognizable word or onomatopoeia should be used. This chanting would represent a form of the human voice from before or after language.

Naomi's song should be rendered as written.

The first two times Naomi is heard, the written text—a series of four "And ...."—should be treated like musical attacks of varying lengths.

In *The Swamp Castle*, Naomi's "And ...." is never meant to be a spoken line, but rather an emphatic beat, punctuating an audible presence.

The Sayings

1. Emerging For The Time Of Sharing   11

2. Traces Of Chaos In The Lasting Home   12

3. Waiting In The Summer Suits   24

4. Night Etchings   28

5. Shock Over The Landscape Box   29

6. The Rubble Of The Un-Coming   33

7. A Yellow Night For The Lastings   36

8. Naomi's Great Machine   40

9. Loving Care Time   45

10. Chasing Ignorance Out Of The Head   47

11. Naomi's Body In The Sky   50

12. Loving Care Time   53

13. And ….   54

14. Three Blind Men In A Closet   56

15. Loving Care Time   59

16. The Out-Of-The-Ordinary Panic   60

17. The Deafness Of The Whole World   69

18. Caulking The Windows To Keep Out The Wind-Dreams   71

19. Lighting The Three-Thousand-Hour Candles   72

20. Moody Waves Break Over The House   78

21. The Swamp Castle   85

21 scenes

THE SAYING:

EMERGING FOR THE TIME OF SHARING

Light increases slowly.

THREE BROTHERS
(ROCK, WILLIAM AND FRED-JAMES)
    Gently, they opened their mouths.

                Gently, dark. Gently, light.

THREE BROTHERS
    Gently, they opened their eyes.

                Gently, dark. Gently, light.

THREE BROTHERS
    Gently, they open their eardrums.

    Always joined-welded together. Always have been.
    Three brothers and a sister joined by an object, the
    same object they hold in their hands: the Say-Sayer.

    Dark.

THE SAYING:

TRACES OF CHAOS IN THE LASTING HOME

ROCK

When they were small, they did not talk. Not one of them. Hardly. Only out of necessity. No need to chatter. The mother, their own, feared this silence.

Loosen them, she said to herself, and to her husband too. Loosen them so we can hear them, so they're audible to this world.

The mother, their own again, thought-dreamed of an object: a game. The father, their own, made it, out of copper.

FRED-JAMES

There you go, children, say something in the Say-Sayer, and you'll get pennies for your piggy banks, said their parents.

WILLIAM

The mother, our own dear mother, bought a picture book; to bring words from our mouths. And for the prettiest words found—a bonus, maybe candy, or some coins.

ROCK

After several years there came the day when it all began, as if, with the Say-Sayer, we had summoned chaos from very far away.

WILLIAM

That day, precisely, the mother, our own, was holding the object.

FRED-JAMES

"Lunchtime, children," and in the sky that noon,
the clouds' black bums were grazing the treetops.

ROCK

Trouble with its lot of sorrow was about to pay us a
visit.

FRED-JAMES

Rock, William and me—Fred-James—and our sister
Naomi, we'd stayed inside all morning. We were
playing cards and with the Say-Sayer, because the
outdoors was too threatening.

WILLIAM

Chaos, I got a bonus for that word, chaos had
started to thunder and flash. On the tin roof of the
house, the rain was hammering drops of iron.

FRED-JAMES

That chaos was dressed like a giant fist with a fierce
wind.

WILLIAM

The father, our own, came in through the door to
the north, bringing with him a gust of wind that
pounded on the door to the south, the front door
that wasn't well latched and flew open in a panic.

FRED-JAMES

You might say our little house was gutted, from
north to south, and if it had been a hurricane-
tornado, we'd all be in the sky to this day.

WILLIAM

The doors were banging furious, the hinges were
screeching, the curtains hanging on for dear life,
the roof was red-hot beneath the pounding drops

of iron, and the father, our mother's beloved, was trying to close the door to the north.

ROCK

I'll help you, pa.

FRED-JAMES

"No, stay with the little ones," he said just before he slid in his wet boots across the waxed wood floor.

WILLIAM

Lightning was striking everywhere. The father, his jaws wide open, was cursing-shouting:

FRED-JAMES

"Close the other door, my wife!" And the mother, her voice like an avalanche, headed for the door to the south, holding the Say-Sayer, screaming: "Stay there, children, all together, welded to one another."

ROCK

The herds of thunder were marching in circles round our tiny house. Thunder as tall as fifty trees, one on top of the other, and as heavy as tons of mountains.

I was the oldest, had to keep the three others attached to my arms. Everything was vibrating, even the little windows in our eyes, the walls of our skin, the cellar of our fears.

WILLIAM

I was screaming: "We have to stay welded together."

Did the mother, our own, mean forever?

ROCK

In the distance, the lightning bolts looked like eighty thousand flashing stilts. Up close, they were crackling with red rage, like blades of knives flaming-burning-pointed-jagged stabbing headfirst at everything that struck their fancy.

WILLIAM

I kept my eyes wide open, my ears closed tight. The father must have shouted once more to his wife:

FRED-JAMES

"Close the doors, we have to stay welded together for eternity."

ROCK

One of the thunderclaps stamped its heel, right there, near the well beside our house, it bent down and sputtered and roared its ugly laughter. Staring right at the father and mother, our own.

The thunder raised its stony arm and grabbed a flashing stilt from the sky and, through the back door still wide open, it hurled the lightning that ripped through the house from stem to stern.

THREE BROTHERS

Like a barbed arrow, the pointed-jagged lightning skewered both hearts in a pell-mell-blood-red-father-mother-blue-flash.

At a time like this, the mother would have said: "When sorrow to a home clings and cloys, mark the morrow for future joys."

A second arrow, unspeakable, passed through the mouth of the Say-Sayer and out came a ball of fire, a ball of fire on fire.

FRED-JAMES

Our little house, even in those days, was out of plumb and that's why the red-red ball rolled out the door and finally fizzled and disappeared into the ground.

ROCK

If you lift the felt carpet, you can see the path of the burn on the creaking floor.

FRED-JAMES

~~Even the copper of the Say-Sayer is stained with a big reddish furrow.~~

~~Recognizable traces, signs of the chaos.~~

WILLIAM

Our wide-eyed faces stared at our parents welded-glued to the nails in the floor.

ROCK

Pleased with their monstrous work, the herds of thunder left bursting their britches from the height of their clouds, showing off for the blades of lightning that were still clowning and winking with glee.

FRED-JAMES

And that was it. Rock, 'cause of the shivers on our skin from the air gone cold in the after-storm, led us-dragged us to the parents' bedroom, to hide under the covers.

ROCK

Naomi, our sister, our youngest, began to scream, holding her head as if she'd received a splinter of electric shock. I should have been nice and consoled her, but her taut voice was yanking on the strings of my nerves, from my scalp to the end of my spine.

I yelled to Fred-James to open the door and to William to come and help me. ~~We threw Naomi out of the room to join our beloved corpses.~~

With our three bodies, we blocked the door. Naomi was still screeching, a real fire siren. And, all of a sudden, another violent blast of thunder struck so loud the breath of the noise shattered every window in the house. We were thrown to the other side of the room.

Naomi, the siren of shipwrecked sailors, had switched off her vocal cords. All we could hear was deep silence.

Straining our ears, we crept to the door, careful not to cut ourselves on the glass.

The unfathomable awaited us.

We saw the father's feet in their boots, the bare arms of the mother, and, pinned-poised at the back of the room, our sister, whose mouth was mauve, her eyes pink, her face drained white, her hair in a fright, her curls turned red.

FRED-JAMES

It must be said: our own little Naomi was floating in the air, suspended, kind of, with a smile on her lips for the three of us. And in her hands, she was holding my father's Saturday night accordion.

WILLIAM

Then she landed like a helicopter. Our little sister began to play and sing. It felt like the song and the wind of the accordion was coming from the pores of her skin, like it was filling the void left by the two dead doors.

ROCK

I shouldn't have made her leave the bedroom, unweld herself from us. Uncontrollable fear.

But we can also say her talent first appeared with the Thunder and the death of the parents.

FRED-JAMES

We dragged the bodies of the father and the mother who were our parents by love, because we all came from different parents unknown to our memories.

They say in early childhood, our bodies were bruised fruits, kind of. That's why the Lasting couple, touched, adopted us to found their family.

The father, our own, is buried to the south, the mother, our mother dear, to the north. Like lightning rods.

WILLIAM

And then, it must be said, we had to sort things out with the municipals. The investigators dispatched by the municipal police, the panicked mayor of the municipality, a devastated coroner, they all came snooping round our house.

What the heck do they all want?

FRED-JAMES

They unburied our Lasting parents, ambulance of the dead, autopsy, interrogation, one right after the other. We all said almost the same thing, depending on if we'd kept our eyes or our ears open.

WILLIAM

That's when we were nicknamed the Ever-Lasting Storms.

ROCK

> They took us to the neighbouring municipality to undergo tests at the little hospital, under the watchful eye of the family doctor, Dr. Blackburn.

WILLIAM

> Him, with a name like that, he should've been a fireman!

FRED-JAMES

> He said: "The three boys are healthy from the ends of their hair to the tip of their big toes. Even Naomi, who's just back from five days of extensive tests at the General Hospital in the Capital, is fine."

WILLIAM

> Five days thinking they'd stolen Naomi away from us. We can't ever unweld again, I kept saying.

ROCK

> Justice left us alone because everything was true. We were even on television, in the papers too.

WILLIAM

> You bet!

ROCK

> Yeah, you! You always loved showin' off.

WILLIAM

> So what, we got everything we asked for.

ROCK

> We have to say it: they tried to take our house away, divide us up, and, especially, separate us from our sister.

> The mayor, Dr. Blackburn's wife, the grocer, the president of the 4H Club and other municipals came to visit us, visit with a purpose, of course.

FRED-JAMES

"Your house is badly insulated," they'd say. "You should all be placed in foster homes. Who's going to take care of little Naomi? You're all so young, who's going to cook?"

WILLIAM

And that Dr. Blackburn who kept plotting to steal Naomi!

ROCK

His wife couldn't have any children. They were dying to adopt a girl, like Naomi.

FRED-JAMES

~~Blackburn even said so during breakfast one day: "If I didn't stop myself, I'd steal her away from you!"~~

WILLIAM

I jump on the table with the jar of honey in my hands.

ROCK

Unrile, William! You can't hit a doctor.

That was when I made my closed decision, dead-bolted. Holding the Say-Sayer in my hands, in front of the Regional Television camera, I declared: "We Lastings aren't movin'. The four of us intend to go on livin' here and goin' to school. As for money, we'll work something out even if we don't know what. We also want our parents to be reburied in the places we chose for them. I'm old enough to hold the reins of the family. Thank you!"

WILLIAM

And me, I'm gonna hold the reins, too. Thank you!

FRED-JAMES

The municipal councillors even held a special
meeting with Dr. Blackburn. Faced with our
stubbornness and Rock's determination, they
passed a resolution to give him their support and
their trust, as long as our behaviour was normal
and logical.

After calling us murderers, the mayor of the
municipality, our uncle, our father's brother,
decided-accepted to help us.

WILLIAM

Help us fill out the government's papers for death
and monetary survival.

ROCK

Help us insulate-paint, glaze-scour the house.

FRED-JAMES

At first, the municipal ladies brought us canned
goods for our weekday meals.

The baker went out of his way to stuff us with bread
and goodies. But it has to be said, he also came to
listen to little Naomi.

WILLIAM

Whirls of jigs for tapping on the waxed floor. Set
the cellar rocking.

We kept going to school by bus, same as always.
The municipal ladies said we were "out of the
ordinary."

Saturday afternoons, while I went with the two little
ones to see the movies in the municipal Rec Hall,
Rock went to the 4H Club to learn how to cook.

FRED-JAMES

As a present for our first Christmas without our parents, we got a big colour TV. It was Mrs. Potter, the president of the 4H Club, who brought it to us.

Everybody calls her Madam See-All because she wants to see everything, know everything, and she's hooked on television, her niece even works for the Regional Television.

ROCK

When we were kids, they organized little parties for us, ten-twelve times a year. Then it was once a year for the three of us, because the fourth, Naomi, once she turned twenty, went away, away from the house and the municipality, to sing.

WILLIAM

Naomi, the tourer of bars in all the surrounding counties, sings of love and pain, in the country-jig or country-crooning style. Once she told us a record company wanted her voice to make her known around the world.

FRED-JAMES

Unexpected, kind of.

ROCK

The unexpected, you can never tell when it will appear. We look all around us, nothing in sight. But right now we're happy because our sister is coming home for the municipal festival, like she promised last year.

We're all ready. We've prepared everything for tomorrow's arrival: beer-done, wine-done, cupcakes-done, stew-done, all-done for our sweet Ginger. Remember when we used to ask her:

FRED-JAMES

"Have you made your bed, Naomi? Done your homework?" She'd answer: "Naomi done. Naomi all-done."

WILLIAM

The joy of seeing her after a whole year. A year! The joy of hearing her.

The Lasting Love Society is going to weld itself together again.

FRED-JAMES

Life has been good to us.

After the whole world's gone to bed,

WILLIAM

we tell our stories, all fidgety-tingly,

ROCK

for the world to come.

The Saying:

Waiting In The Summer Suits

Fred-James

Fred-James told William Rock's advice: they should stand straight, proud, their arms open, for the greeting . And say, at her first glance, welcome, to their sister.

William

It's eight in the morning, we're in our Sunday best. Today we won't dare sit down, anywhere. We brush off flecks of dust, blow away pollen, we stay new, brand new.

Even the sky is new.

Fred-James

What a perfect day for waiting! With my heart beating so loud it almost buries my voice. From head to toe, when I'm dressed up fancy, I feel taller, like the Christmas-fancy feeling, in our winter holiday suits, but today, we're standing tall in our summer suits.

A clean shave, skin all pink, we patted our cheeks with the summer perfume. We change perfume with the seasons. The bottle of winter perfume is tucked away in the cedar-made closet packed to the brim: "Don't open till the first snowfall."

Sweet-smelling like when we go, once a month, to see the girls from the Capital, the big city girls. They come to dance in the other bar in the municipality; our little nights out, to untease that

24

itch and life's humdrum, with Josie, Hortense, Mimi and company. I'm thinking about those girls too, while we wait for our Naomi.

Waiting.

Noontime, we take off our jackets, we wash our still clean hands, undo our cufflinks, roll up our sleeves, carefully up to our elbows, and we tuck our ties into our shirts. Rock and William, they put on bibs. We stand away from the counter, we prepare our tomato and lettuce sandwiches with mayonnaise dribbling over the crusts, and we eat, still standing, leaning over the table, eyeing each other.

ROCK

Don't move, Fred-James!

Go wash my hands, clean his damn spot. I told you to put a dishtowel around your neck ... no, I won't get nothing on me ... now look at you!

FRED-JAMES

Each one gets a glass of pop, one packaged cupcake, to save the fresh "cupcakes-done."

Wash our hands, then, redo it all in reverse so we can go back outside, all new, each of us with his fifty-six ways of waiting.

WILLIAM

I'll spend the afternoon leaning against the van all polished-wax shiny. When we bought it, Rock of course chose the model with no extras, me, the pretty red colour and Fred-James, the name: The Bull.

When Naomi comes down the road, I'll wait to make my impression, 'cause Rock, with his bad habits of the oldest, will make the first move, for sure, and Fred-James will flutter right over to Naomi like a humming-bird. Then, I'll stick my arm through the open window and I'll make The Bull's horn shout, like at wedding parties. That's when she'll see me, she'll walk toward me, and me toward her. We'll stand still, my fingers will pinch her cheeks: hello, hello, my pretty Ginginge!

ROCK

When she comes inside, I'll show her what's left of the cassette. Last time she came to visit, we spent a whole afternoon in the house recording her voice and her music.

Look, little bits of twisted tape. We're real sorry. 'Cause of a fight between the three of us. A bashing-bruising. We only had one copy of your voice because we never thought such a thing would happen. I'm gonna rent the machines again 'cause every time you go away, we end up forgetting your voice. This time we'll make a good supply so we never lose you again.

FRED-JAMES

A whole day without sitting down, pacing back and forth. Then suppertime, repeating the same routine as at lunch. The whole evening waiting, waiting in front of the TV, and taking turns going outside to check with the flashlight.

ROCK

Wondering why she didn't come when she promised and why all year not a single telephone number to reach her, why?

Whispering to our third ear the worst horror
stories. I prepare myself because, because sometimes it happens.

WILLIAM
The three of us, silent, worrying ourselves to death.

FRED-JAMES
Such much waiting for no arrival!

After the evening, the night settled in on our little
house and around the TV. We fell asleep, not on
purpose, in our summer suits.

THE SAYING:

NIGHT ETCHINGS

ROCK

Rock told himself not to fret, to get some sleep. In the middle of the night, sobs wake him up.

I drag myself out of bed. The other nights, I searched the dark, with my night eyes, to see if one of my brothers was whining in his sleep. No, after a long silence, they even started to snore.

Who's sobbing with that gaping hole in his voice? It's hollow, hollow, the pain of those sobs.

I even go outdoors with the flashlight taking glimpses. Shadows swirl around the ray of light trying to scare me, that's when I think that trouble is lurking round the house and that some day, it's going to sit down on the roof and smash everything. I feel so small, like a field cricket singing in the night.

I just heard it again, tonight. I took the time to listen to it, without getting upset, especially without moving, so the sounds would continue.

It's me, it's me who's crying! It's my voice.

What is it crying about?

I don't have time to console that voice, not yet.

THE SAYING:

SHOCK OVER THE LANDSCAPE BOX

ROCK

> Rock said, while they were watching a war movie on
> television, that he had talked to their uncle, the
> mayor, about not expecting them, not them or
> Naomi, at the municipal festival. Rock added that
> they were upset about their sister not arriving and
> that, if she was not back in a month, they were
> going to register their worry officially with the
> police force.

WILLIAM

> How can you say that's a real war? It's all made up.
> Played by actors.

ROCK

> Yeah, but it's the story of a real war that ended
> about twenty years ago.

WILLIAM

> You clown! Your damn news is just more stories
> made up by the TV big wigs.

ROCK

> What are you saying there?! C'mon, don't tell me
> you don't see the difference!

WILLIAM

> Don't you realize that everything that comes out of
> there, it's just ways of cooking up beliefs that make
> no darn sense.

Wake up, brother, or your fears'll get worse 'n
worse and you'll die a horrible death.

ROCK

Unbelievable!

WILLIAM

You said it, unbelievable!

Abruptly dark. Beat. Abruptly light.

FRED-JAMES

Hurry, William! The girls must've started dancin',
don't wanta miss the show.

WILLIAM

Coming. Rock, you gonna tape the movie for us?

FRED-JAMES

Thanks for stayin' home, case Naomi arrives. It will
untease the itch for sure ... I reserved Mimi!

WILLIAM

Whoopee-doo! Mimi!

ROCK

Hey, William, don't tell the girls your ideas about
TV; we'll keep that between ourselves, okay?

WILLIAM

Look, pops, tomorrow night it'll be your turn to
untease your whoopee-doo with Hortense.

FRED-JAMES

Whoopee-doo!

Abruptly dark. Beat. Abruptly light.

WILLIAM

Fred-James, your big brother thinks they went to
make movies in space with their whole kit and

kaboodle. Rock, those movies, they're not acted by
ordinary guys, those are real actors.

FRED-JAMES
Travel to outer space! Poor Rock!

ROCK
Stop clownin' around! Those men really are in
their shuttle circlin' round the earth, the earth is in
a universe, our universe is next to other universes.
Wake up! We've already walked on the moon!

WILLIAM
You think you're smarter than the rest of us, just so
you can say the opposite. The moon—you ever take
a good look?!

FRED-JAMES
Right, the moon!

WILLIAM
Go stand by the window. Now, Rock, lean over. You
see the difference between your brother's foot and
the moon! C'mon, can you see your kid brother
walkin' on a tiny thing like that?

FRED-JAMES
That's the voice of common sense.

ROCK
Stop horsin' around and come dry the dishes.

WILLIAM
Good, I think he finally got the picture!

Abruptly dark. Beat. Abruptly light.

FRED-JAMES

Enough to make you sick, sick to your stomach!
Goddamn bigmouth wiseguy. Wake up, Rock! We
just got home from the big city girls.

WILLIAM

Last month, when it was your turn to go see
Hortense, you two plotted a little lesson for the two
of us, right?

Josie refused to get undressed till I said the same
things you believe about TV.

FRED-JAMES

Me too, you damn blabbermouth, I lied through
my teeth to have Mimi. You make me sick to my
stomach. We don't wanta believe all that stuff, you
hear?

WILLIAM

We'll stop goin' to see them, if that's the way it's
gonna be. Make me feel stupid, dammit!

ROCK

Okay, guys, I'll let them know.

FRED-JAMES

If it was true, Rock, can you imagine the shock it
would put in people's heads?!

WILLIAM

For once and for all, those are actors, not ordinary
guys 'cause they do things that ain't ordinary!

Slowly, dark.

THE SAYING:

THE RUBBLE OF THE UN-COMING

ROCK
  Rock, when he was little, once read out loud on a
  box: Society Tea Biscuits—The Pleasure of Sharing.
  That's what gave him the idea of writing on the Say-
  Sayer box: The Lasting Society Say-Sayer: The
  Pleasure of Sharing.
  Wake up, The Lasting Society! Look who's come
  home.

WILLIAM
  At last, at last!

FRED-JAMES
  Yes, at long last-last!

ROCK
  The three of us, at the window, the curtains pulled-
  parted.

WILLIAM
  Without budging, watching Naomi come down the
  road with two unknown armholders and a third
  one carrying her little suitcase and her accordion. 3 extra People

FRED-JAMES
  'Cause of the wobbly way she was walking, and her
  mouth hanging open, her topsy-turvy eyes, one of
  the guys who saw us staring at them through the
  window says: "We found her in a telephone booth,
  she'd been holed up there for two days. Better have
  her put away."

Waving the broom handle unscrewed like a
warning, Rock went out to tell them to leave.

ROCK

I'll kill them for getting our sister tipsy like that!

WILLIAM

Me too!

The guys let go of Naomi: A landslide. Nothing
held together on its own. A pile of rubble. Our
sister spilled over the ground. Swinging doors
banged in our hearts.

ROCK

They managed to get into their car before we beat
them to a pulp.

WILLIAM

They took off before we pounded their hood in.

ROCK

Take a whiff of her mouth, heartless girl.

FRED-JAMES

Phew, sure don't smell like roses.

WILLIAM

No news for a year! Bitch. We said too many nice
things about you. We should strike a match in your
ass, fire would come out of your mouth.

ROCK

We could shout our worry-upset at both sides of
your head, right into your deafness. Can you hear
that?

FRED-JAMES

But we won't do it this time, bad Ginginge, right,
Rock?

ROCK

We'll see. Right now, the rest of the Society is going inside. ~~Let her get untipsy by herself.~~

Drunk

The Saying:
A Yellow Night For The Lastings

FRED-JAMES

Fred-James said it didn't make sense leaving Naomi
to suffer all day at the end of the road. Fred-James
is afraid of making Rock angry: if Rock decides he
is going to let her dry out, right there on the
ground for days and days, he will do it, there is no
changing his mind, a closed decision, dead-bolted.
Once Rock left William begging outside the door
for six days.

When the sun was leaving to spend the day
somewhere else, the big brothers went out to look
at her, panic in the back of their eyes.

Does she look like she's untipsy?

ROCK

Hey, the swooner, not so close.

WILLIAM

A little touch, can't tell much.

ROCK

Nothing but her accordion and her empty suitcase.
Incomprehensible!

WILLIAM

Maybe those guys who drove her here robbed her.
Or maybe not, figure it out.

ROCK

You think she smells of booze?

WILLIAM

Not really. Just looks dead drunk 'cause nothing's moving. Smells more like piss. Should we take her inside?

ROCK

Get a hold of yourself, Naomi. Stop spillin' all over.

FRED-JAMES

Nice of you to bring her inside.

WILLIAM

Shut up! Come help us carry her.

FRED-JAMES

Naomi still seems tipsy. We lift her up, we carry her. We climb the stairs to the south, and, right on the doorstep, an unexpected ... fit. Her legs, her arms, every which way. Heavy breathing. Her heart trying to leap out of her chest, kind of. We dropped her, we all fell over.

All three brothers, voiceless, try, a third, a fifth time, and every time, on the doorstep, a thrashing, enough to knock them down the stairs.

ROCK

Fred-James, go get the Say-Sayer.

WILLIAM

My lip's cut. Crazy bitch! Ginginge on a binge!

ROCK

William, watch your language in front of your sister.

Say it into the Say-Sayer, why this fit, Naomi?

WILLIAM

What's wrong, Ginginge?

If somebody gave you a boo-boo, I'll go tear his guts out with my teeth, I swear.

FRED-JAMES

We waited, not knowing what to do. When night had settled in the sky, we set her up on the porch, with her feather pillow and her blanket from the old days.

We turned on the outdoor lights, the yellow anti-bug bulbs. And us, from the other side of the screen door, we watched her, sipping on our hot chocolate, even though it wasn't winter; a little treat to soothe our panic.

Abruptly dark. Abruptly light.

FRED-JAMES

In the morning, the sun came back to chase the night away, we hadn't budged.

ROCK

She's not gettin' untipsy.

WILLIAM

Just say it: the flies are buzzing round 'er 'cause it stinks somethin' awful!

ROCK

Almost indecent, not to take care of her.

FRED-JAMES

The getting untipsy would happen if we took care of her like a baby: wash her, dress her, give her something to eat and drink.

ROCK

Yeah, all that, and then what? Fred-James, first get her a drink of water, her tongue is thick.

WILLIAM
Yoo-hoo, hello, sweet Ginginge! We're gonna
pamper you, show you how much we love you.

FRED-JAMES
Welcome home!

WILLIAM
Welcome home, Ginginge!

ROCK
Welcome home, anyway, sweet Ginginge.

THE SAYING:

NAOMI'S GREAT MACHINE

WILLIAM

William told his uncle, to prevent him from getting out of his truck, that Naomi was fine, just a bit tired. And his uncle, like every time he sees the yard, offered to send a municipal truck to help neaten up their junk.

Why bug us, eh? We already told you: no throwin' away our odds and ends, never know when they might come in handy. Bye, now. I got work to do. Proof: the rusty bathtub, full of rain, we emptied it, derusted-painted it, just like new. We set it up between two clotheslines, and hung blankets up for privacy.

Naomi's outdoors bathtub!

ROCK

We'll clean the crud from between your toes. You'll feel better after.

William! Stop that, you pig!

WILLIAM

What's buggin' you?

ROCK

Why are you stickin' your fingers there?

WILLIAM

I'm cleanin' her up.

ROCK

You're fiddlin' with her!

WILLIAM

I'm cleanin' her, with love.

Besides, who says she's my sister? We don't know
where we come from.

FRED-JAMES

Naomi, she's the lasting-love sister of all three of us.

ROCK

Stop your useless tongue-wagging or I'll knock your
front teeth out.

WILLIAM

Go get our real birth certificates. For each of us.
Proof before the law. If I wanted, she could be my
wife.

FRED-JAMES

Don't say that, William, don't say stuff like that.

WILLIAM

Different bodies, different faces, nobody's the same
here.

ROCK

You goddamn Ever-Lasting Storm!

I chase him, grab him by the hair, throw him on
the ground.

WILLIAM

Unrile, Rock, unrile! I don't want to marry
Ginginge, you crazy?!

ROCK

We know we don't come from the same vagina,
what difference does that make?

WILLIAM

I'm right,though.

ROCK

Goddam empty skull! And you, Fred-James, unswoon!

WILLIAM

Stop tryin' to control everything we do.

FRED-JAMES

Don't say that, William. We are the same, the Lasting Love Society.

Come here, my two brothers, and powder-dry our sister.

WILLIAM

I went to fetch the old harness we'd used for a horse that got too old to lie down. He didn't have the strength to pull himself up, so we'd put the harness on him and let him sleep standing.

We strapped the old harness to the machine we invented for Naomi.

FRED-JAMES

When we were kids, we had built, in the little woods at the end of our land, a miniature castle with some leftover cement and fieldstones. We promised Naomi that when she got married we would build her a real one. If she found her wedding prince today, we couldn't build it there because even her little castle is flooded in the swamp.

But we built her a great machine so we can take good care of her.

ROCK

Now we can sit her down, hold her up, lie her down and slide her into the bathtub. Next time, we'll feed her first and we'll wash-scrub her after, right after.

WILLIAM

Sweet Ginginge! You're not goin' to the hospital, we'll save you with our loving care, the lasting love of your loving brothers.

It looks like she's smilin'.

ROCK

Hold on! Where were you gonna set up her machine?

WILLIAM

Next to the house, out front.

ROCK

Ha! Out front! Empty skull! How smart are we gonna look leavin' our sister harnessed to a machine lit by one lousy bulb?

WILLIAM

Goddamn bigmouth wiseguy! Who do you think you are?

ROCK

We have to be careful. It's gettin' late, we'll decide where to put her tomorrow.

FRED-JAMES

Mad, William stomps into the house saying: I'm gonna stop talkin', so he'll stop pissin' me off.

Rock following him inside answers: Good, 'cause I'm fed up listenin' to you.

William, he decides to go straight to bed, and shouts: Fuck off.

And Rock: Right.

William again: Shithead!

And Rock: Shut your trap, goddam pig!

William: Shut yours, it's your asshole.

Rock: Right, good night anyway, William.

William: Ungood night.

We all went to bed.

WILLIAM
Rock, Rock ... you asleep?

ROCK
Yes, I'm asleep!

WILLIAM
Okay ... I say we put Naomi behind the house, but we better make a porthole-window in the door to the north, just to keep an eye on her.

ROCK
We'll make your porthole-window. Stop worryin' bout it, good night, brother.

WILLIAM
Yeah, good night, brother. Good night, Fred-James. Good night, Naomi.

FRED-JAMES
Sometimes I think about our ages. I know our four ages really well, but it's like we have two ages at the same time: old as the hills with the eyes of children.

> *Gradual dark. In the total darkness, NAOMI appears phosphorescent.*

THE SAYING:
LOVING CARE TIME

ROCK

Rock told his Hortense, his favourite whoopee-doo
love-lady, to bring him some magazines with
unnude women; magazines for understanding
women's stuff. Rock went to the other bar to pick
up the supplies. There must have been at least ten
thousand of them, almost filled The Bull with
paper. We set Fred-James up with the reading.

I asked William to build a workbench with soft-
feeling boards on the top because Dr. Blackburn
told me we would have to massage our sister so her
muscles wouldn't atrophy.

Take it easy, William! Like dancin' with your hands.
Use more oil, don't want to hurt her. Good, now
turn her over. Careful! Like this.

WILLIAM

Naomi's bleeding! We're gonna kill her with your
halfwitted dancin'.

Scared crazy, we took off with Naomi bare-naked in
the The Bull.

ROCK

I was driving, I drove straight to Blackburn's house.
His wife says he isn't home. I tell her about our
sister, she runs to the The Bull. My two brothers are
fighting, sitting on the spare tire. She examines
Naomi and asks me to lift up my sister's legs.

Shut your traps! Madam Blackburn has something to say.

FRED-JAMES

Oh! So that's what periods are! I read about it, but that's not the way I imagined it.

ROCK

The doctor's wife showed us how to put a pad on. And she told us we'd have to buy a kind of diaper for her incontinence. We shouted, thanks, thanks, and took off fast 'cause she looked like she might want to come with us.

We stopped at the pharmacy. On the road home, I told William with a little grin: Okay this can be your job.

THE SAYING:

CHASING IGNORANCE OUT OF THE HEAD

FRED-JAMES

Fred-James told William to come take a look at
Rock who was busy talking to Dr. Blackburn. He
had come to stethoscope Naomi who was out of her
machine.

WILLIAM

What the heck is he doin', feelin' our sister up like
that? He couldn't adopt her, so now he wants to
marry her?

FRED-JAMES

Don't make a fuss! Look, he's finished, he's leavin'.

WILLIAM

So what did roach face have to say?

ROCK

He's disappointed with us. He says our sister's not
doin' very well and that our care doesn't meet the
standards.

WILLIAM

Can't the old fart mind his own business?

ROCK

It's our uncle, the genius, who sent him. Dr.
Blackburn said I should take Naomi to the General
Hospital.

FRED-JAMES

All the way to the Capital! Why can't you just go to
the little hospital?

ROCK

They don't have the equipment to do some kind of ~~special head x-rays~~. And while she's there, they'll do some blood and urine tests—

WILLIAM

~~Urine, urine,~~ he should go screw himself, that one.

Doctors think they know everything with all their great knowledge. But they'll never understand what she is.

~~Put the Say-Sayer on the table so we can talk about it.~~

ROCK

~~Lay off, William.~~

WILLIAM

I was against lettin' her leave with the dirty old baker. He convinced her he could be her money manager for tourin' the bars. Bastard dropped her, two years later, for a singer who paid more.

Naomi went on singin' all over creation, and you approved of it, you were all for freedom, let her see the world! Not me! I knew those damn smoky tours would wear her body out. It's the fresh air around here that'll put her back on her feet, not your doctors.

ROCK

I'm leavin' tomorrow and there's no changin' my mind, a closed decision, dead-bolted.

FRED-JAMES

Better go shoppin' before you leave, nothin' left in the house to eat.

ROCK

Just tests, William. We can't allow Ginginge to go on like this, in a fog, for centuries on end!

WILLIAM

I'm warnin' you, Rock Lasting, if you leave Naomi in the arms of medicine, I'll beat you to a pulp.

The Saying:

Naomi's Body In The Sky

WILLIAM
> After two weeks of no news from Rock, William
> said: waiting is horrible for the heart. His anger
> spread to his kid brother's nerves, until he was just
> as mad. By the morning Rock and Naomi returned,
> the brothers had eaten all the supplies.
>
> At last, at last!

FRED-JAMES
> Yeah, at long last-last.
>
> Fool! Don't you know your own telephone
> number?

WILLIAM
> You got no heart, no brains! We been holdin' our
> breath for two weeks.

ROCK
> Hey! Undo your nerves! Say hello to Ginginge.

WILLIAM
> Mad as a horsefly, I attack my brother.

ROCK
> Naomi, strapped in her rented chair, must have
> seen me grab Fred-James by the collar and shake
> him out of his anger-swoon; she must have seen
> William, too, swinging his fists and baring his fangs
> at me.

50

With the back of my hand, I get William in the head, Fred-James falls on the ground shaking. I feint and catch William in a bear hug.

I knew that while we were gone our brothers had been worried-scared out of their wits.

FRED-JAMES
Worrying sick leaves an awful taste, and out of my swooning mouth I spit a warped sound: Mama.

ROCK
Unrile, William, unrile.

WILLIAM
We thought death had snatched you away from life, or that you'd run away forever with Ginginge.

ROCK
William and Fred-James were on the ground crying like babies. After a while, they calmed down, I pulled them close together, side-by-side. I went to get our sister and pushed her right up to their twisted-grimace faces. I'd brought back some chewing gum for driving, and an envelope full of x-rays and scan-rays of Naomi.

I showed them the medical pictures. The four of us, lying on the ground, welded together, chewing away, we looked up at the sky, our arms stretched out, holding in our hands the interior photos of our sister.

WILLIAM
That's what our Ginginge has inside her head?

ROCK
Yes, a blood clot stuck in her brain.

FRED-JAMES

Can't they remove a red-red clot?

ROCK

The doctors say the risk is so great she might never come back.

WILLIAM

'Cause maybe she can become the old Ginginge again?

ROCK

They say the chances are slight. One thing's for sure, I think the risk is too great to let them operate.

FRED-JAMES

But William and me, we thought those x-rays were beautiful to look at, 'cause in the sky, our sister seemed to be floating on the inside with the clouds.

ROCK

Peace restored. Trying to console your brothers' fear, when that fear flows deep in the blood, it's harder than building a castle, if you ask me.

THE SAYING:

LOVING CARE TIME

FRED-JAMES

Fred-James said he was going to the pharmacy, to
the beauty counter, to buy a good makeup kit.

WILLIAM

Poor Fred-James! No need to read ten thousand
magazines to know that Naomi would have got rid
of those little hairs on her face.
We can shave Ginginge with nice shaving cream
and brand new blades. You're gonna look real
pretty! Every morning, I'll do yours after mine, it's
no big deal!

FRED-JAMES

Moron, you want to disfigure her? Push over, you
dummy. I bought some de-pil-a-tory cream.

WILLIAM

Stop actin' like Rock, givin' orders! If you ask me,
you're turnin' into a real fuss-budget.

FRED-JAMES

I read all about it in the magazines. Girl stuff, it's
not the same as for guys.

WILLIAM

Where did you get that colour?

FRED-JAMES

Our sister used to look like a star, her makeup has
to be à la mode.

THE SAYING:

AND....

ROCK
And, constantly, carefully, the Lasting brothers work
their labour of love for their sister.

FRED-JAMES
And sometimes, even, they stand stock still beside
Naomi's machine and let the sun and the moon
circle round them, three times, kind of.

WILLIAM
And when darkness falls, they gather up their
sister's loving care accessories and William lowers
the felt mat to cover the machine.

ROCK
And one night, the Lastings go into the house, they
eat and go to bed with raindrops on the tin roof
that put them to sleep like bears.

FRED-JAMES
And in the middle of the night, a thunderclap high
in the sky wakes Rock. And he listens.

NAOMI
And....
And....
And....
And....

ROCK

And anxious, Rock goes to shake his brothers'
sleeping shoulders.

WILLIAM

And through the porthole-window, coming from
behind the mats, they see a strange glow.

FRED-JAMES

And their raincoats over their heads, in their
nightclothes, they walk over to the machine and
discover that their sister's skin is luminous.

THE SAYING:

THREE BLIND MEN IN A CLOSET

ROCK

Rock said to go to Naomi's very-own cedar-made closet, and find, in the left-behind things, a nightgown transparent enough to see if her whole body became luminous.

FRED-JAMES

Once when she was little, Naomi had a sleep-walking dream. In the middle of the night, she opened her closet door and saw her three brothers gone blind. For nights after, Naomi was afraid to fall asleep.

To settle her fear, our mother wrote on the door: "The blind men are gone."

WILLIAM

What could we write on the roof of our house to get rid of our fear?

ROCK

"Our sister is getting better."

WILLIAM

Let's just say, Ginginge, that loving-care cures everything.

FRED-JAMES

We couldn't find anything in the closet so I dragged out our mother's old sewing machine and I sewed all day long, very slowly, so I wouldn't make any mistakes. I managed to make a pretty nice

nightgown out of some sheer curtains. I needed
four windows to dress her.

WILLIAM

Naomi, tonight we're gonna cook supper on the
outside grill. Tonight we gonna watch over you.
We're not gonna cover up your machine. When you
light up, we'll move closer so we can hear you sing.
Sing to tell us: I'm getting better.

ROCK

Darkness falls, my brothers are sleeping.

Night has covered the sky with an old felt mat,
quite thick but very worn, so worn the light from
the sun, still there on the other side, taking a break
from our monkey mugs, shines through some of
the holes.

I didn't wake the little Society when my sister lit up.

Is the sun shining beneath your eyes, my brothers?
Is the sun shining beneath my eyes when I'm
sleeping?
Is the sun shining beneath your eyes, Naomi?

You don't sing anymore, you don't talk anymore.
Can you hear us, can you see us?

Maybe in your heart of hearts, you're building
yourself a castle of light. Maybe you're preparing
rooms for us, so we can come live with you. Maybe
that's where I'll cure my tears, there in your castle
of light. Maybe we'll be free in our bodies, maybe
we'll be free in our hearts. Maybe all the sorrow
clinging to our home will become the joys of
tomorrow. Maybe you promised to marry the
Thunder that came when you were little. Then
we'd be brothers-in-law to the Thunder.

If your mouth married the thundering sky, we'd go to your wedding. Big rumbling chariots would bounce over the dented clouds, you'd leave on your honeymoon with cans rattling from the fenders.

We'd drink a shower of beer and soda and spiked punch; our tongues would be loosened and we'd talk, we'd sing with the glowing sky.

Good night, Ginginge.

The Saying:

Loving Care Time

ROCK

Rock said to William: did you see the price?

WILLIAM

The other body lotion, the one you bought, stunk
awful. Who cares how much it costs if it makes her
smell good!

ROCK

We've got enough now!

Last month we skipped going to see the girls, we'll
have to skip it again this month. There's a limit to
what we can spend!

FRED-JAMES

Rock, it can't hurt, it might lead her to the road to
recovery.

Look how pretty I've made her. Eh, Ginginge! A
nice manicure, her nails all trimmed-painted, her
hair all cut-curled. And her face! All tweezered-and-
made-up.

Look at yourself in the mirror, Ginginge. Say it,
Rock, tell her she's as pretty as she was before, it'll
make her happy.

WILLIAM

And she smells good. Say it, Rock, say it to the
Lasting Love Society.

ROCK

Our sister is the most beautiful in the whole world.

THE SAYING:

THE OUT-OF-THE-ORDINARY PANIC

WILLIAM
> William said, after he had brought in the wood for the winter, dug up the garden, prepared the The Bull for the snow, that they had to discuss their sister's future.
>
> The three brothers, their throats filled with sobs, admitted to each other that their loving care hadn't improved Naomi's condition. William cried for an hour his head on the table.
>
> They decided to bring her inside before the autumn arrived.

ROCK
> First, inside the house, we decorated her own comfy loving-care corner. When the time came, she let us bring her in without a fuss or a struggle.
>
> A month later, when I was clearing the table, I told William: this afternoon, Dr. Blackburn called.

WILLIAM
> Not him again!

FRED-JAMES
> Let's talk about it some other time.

ROCK
> Don't start swooning, Fred-James! Feed your sister instead.

WILLIAM

We're never gonna let her go live with strangers in some institution.

ROCK

Listen, before you blow a gasket. Dr. Blackburn went himself to discuss the test results with the doctors at the General Hospital. They could attempt a laser operation.

WILLIAM

Never, Rock! Never!

ROCK

Dr. Blackburn says we're cruel with our methods of carin' for her. He told me again that he could ask Public Health to take Naomi out of our custody.

WILLIAM

He wants to kill us!

ROCK

This would be the last chance for the doctors.

WILLIAM

Has your heart become an enemy of the Lastings? At the hardware store, I saw Madam See-All and she whispered that this summer, her and her husband, they saw our sister lookin' like she was all lit up. I said it was 'cause of the kind of lightbulbs we use.

You see, that's proof our sister is out-of-the-ordinary. Not everyone lights up like that! But, Mr. Rock, who knows better than everybody, he wants to turn her over to those bloody scavengers.

ROCK

Dr. Blackburn insisted, he says with the new equipment they could have a sixty percent chance of saving Naomi.

FRED-JAMES

Anyway, that proves ~~we're not the only ones who see her light up~~.

WILLIAM

It's a lot of love that's gonna bring our sister back. We havta be even ~~purer in our hearts to give her nothing but love, love~~.

Besides, the doctors they don't know nothing about medicine. Take my case—

ROCK

The unexpected. Is that the unexpected knocking at our door again?

I go to the door. Nothing.

For a second, I thought sorrow had just entered our home.

FRED-JAMES

Let's stop talkin' about this, brothers, I can't feed Naomi when I'm upset.

ROCK

William, it's not Sunday. Havta put the beer away.

WILLIAM

Says who, I helped make this beer.

You want to forget my medical case!

With our black and brown leather skates, we'd gone skating for the first time together on the little pond down the road. I yelled to you: don't leave me alone. You were makin' circles round me 'cause you already knew how to skate ... this is how you skate, William, like this ... I was screamin' ... just watch what I can do, smart ass.

62

I made a beeline for the back of the pond. You were laughin' and shoutin': you're skatin' on your ankles.

I spin around too fast, furious, to shout at you: get lost! My legs get twisted, I had a hundred arms flying-trying to keep my balance but my big trap was pullin' me forward, and boom!, a split chin. Get back to the house by the snowy road, leavin' a trail of blood. And you, instead of consolin' me, you were bangin' your fist on my shoulder 'cause you can't stand it when somebody gets hurt, it cramps your style.

The father took me to emergency. And who was on duty? The torturer, Dr. Blackburn who had to freeze me to sew the stitches. His goddamn needle hit a nerve. My whole face was frozen. I couldn't talk for the life of me. Blackburn, goddamn face-breaker, he never figured out why the shot lasted two years. Two years, messed up like that!

I'm not about to forget his roach face.

FRED-JAMES

I was too little to go skating, but I went to see the drops of blood on the snow.

ROCK

C'mon, William, put the beer away!

WILLIAM

Tell us what you think, Fred-James! Say something, Rock will listen to you.

FRED-JAMES

I must say, if she stays like that, tipsy her whole life, and we keep her forever, we've gotta fix up the house for convenience. And we'll have to—

ROCK

William, you're getting on my nerves. You're
wasting our supplies.

WILLIAM

I don't give a shit about your damn rules and
regulations.

ROCK

You can buzz like a horsefly all you want, but I've
decided to try the operation, a closed decision,
dead-bolted.

WILLIAM

My sonofabitch of a brother thinks he's in
command of the world army. Operation, operation,
you wanta see the kinda operation I'm gonna give
you?

I break the bottle, the beer pours onto the floor.
He's bleeding before he can open his trap.

I'm hurtin' you so you'll bleed to death.

FRED-JAMES

Rock!

WILLIAM

William ain't gonna bite his tongue no more. Rock,
the oldest Lasting brother, ain't gonna play leader
no more. It's all over, finished. When I was little,
you were my hero, but that's all over now.

ROCK

William—

WILLIAM

I can still hear you gasping.

And me yellin' at you: gasp, choke, die.

Another blast of anger makes me lift you off the
ground and bang your head against the cupboard
doors.

Hear that, the dishes are shakin'!

I was killing him. Blood kept pouring down his
neck.

Fred-James, both hands reaching for the ceiling,
like he wanted to unscrew the lightbulbs, was
shouting:

FRED-JAMES
Calm down, William, we're Lasting love brothers.

Have you forgotten about love?

WILLIAM
You can stuff our Love Society in your mouth and
brush your teeth with it.

FRED-JAMES
Stop makin' him suffer.

WILLIAM
Don't touch him or I'll give you a taste of the same
medicine.

Listen, Rock, I'm tellin' you for the first time, I
hate the way you talk with your hands, the way you
move with your body, the way you listen with your
head, the way you think with your eyes. I hate all
your ways.

I havta say it: we don't look alike in our faces, it's
worse than that, we look alike in our way of being,
in all our ways. Not even the municipals can tell us
apart, as long as we don't talk.

When you comb your hair like that, I do too, always
have, naturally, but now, if I see myself make a

single gesture, I don't care what, if it reminds me of you and I feel like I'm you, I'll go wash my hands to erase you. I want to invent my self, without you being there to order me around. I don't want to see you in my gestures anymore.

Looking like you, a terrible atrocity for my skull.

I'm not as dumb as you think. Some day I'll show you who I am. Show everybody what I'm capable of. Incredible things, Rock, incredible things, you can't even imagine.

Fred-James, you swooner, take the tablecloth off your sister's head.

FRED-JAMES

We can't let her see that. Good grief, we've come to bloodshed!

ROCK

Hospital ... my ... bro ...

WILLIAM

When I was ten, I wrote on the red cardboard on the dictionary: "My brother Rock is crazy." Even young, a damn decider! Don't ever call me your brother again.

FRED-JAMES

He's bleeding so hard, in the puddle of his blood, we can see the reflection of the inside of the house.

Let's stay welded!

William, we gotta go to emergency.

WILLIAM

First, Mr. Rock is gonna swear to the Love Society: Naomi, here present, will stay in the Lasting Home.

And no changin' my mind, a closed decision of
William Lasting, dead-bolted.

ROCK
Yesss.

FRED-JAMES
Yes. He said yes.

WILLIAM
Yes, who, what?

ROCK
Ginge … stays, Y'am says.

WILLIAM
Ginginge stays, Y'am says. Attaboy, my Rock.

I start to bawl: Now, Rock Lasting, we'll take you to
emergency, but I'm warnin' you, from now on,
you're not the only one makin' decisions about life
around here.

FRED-JAMES
I bring the The Bull in front of the house, we open
the doors and slide Rock onto the old mattress that
smells of rot …

At times like this, our mother would have said:
"When sorrow to a home clings and cloys, mark the
morrow for future joys."

I talk to Rock about the girls he likes while we
drive.

WILLIAM
That's right, talk to him about Hortense, it'll keep
him alive. And tell him to stay welded.

I was bawling and blinking, trying to see where I
was headed.

We get to the emergency of the little hospital. That night, sad to say, it's the butcher Blackburn on duty again with his gobbledygook white jacket talk.

I told him: don't paralyse his face or I'll come back and tear your eyes out.

His hands were shaking when he sewed up the cut. Bastard wanted to keep Rock overnight. They say we took off fast: you won't get our brother alive!

FRED-JAMES

We drove home along a misty fall road. In the house filled with darkness, we found Ginginge all lit up, lying on the floor next to the puddle of blood.

The Saying:
The Deafness Of The Whole World

FRED-JAMES

Fred-James told William: Rock's been running a
fever for three days now. With panic in his voice,
Fred-James went to get Dr. Blackburn. William
found work to do in the garage while Dr. Blackburn
changed the bandage on Rock's wound. He gave
me a prescription for pills for the pain. I thought
he'd talk a lot more, he hardly said a thing.

At first, Rock can't talk, the broken glass cut close
to the vocal cords. Four days later, he starts to get
better. He even got up, washed, shaved and ate. He
wrote: find me a nice red scarf.

Our uncle came during your fever, his mouth full
of insults, because of the blood, our being scared at
emergency, shouting that we'd become the shame
of the municipality. He ended with: "Bunch of
thunderstruck retards."

WILLIAM

"Goddamn pretentious municipal creep," I shouted
back.

Rock, when you start talking again, you have to
chew him out, that one, he's lost respect for the
Lastings.

FRED-JAMES

Rock writes: nothing to say bout that. It's ready,
come eat.

69

WILLIAM

Go ahead, watch your damn world news during our meal.

I'm not eating, it tastes of sour grapes!

FRED-JAMES

Rock writes: no grapes, look at your plate!

WILLIAM

With your mug full of reproach, everything tastes of sour grapes.

FRED-JAMES

Rock writes: I've always put love into my cooking.

WILLIAM

It's my closed decision, dead-bolted, that's spread reproach over your face, say it, say it to the whole world.

FRED-JAMES

Rock writes: the whole world is deaf.

CAULKING THE WINDOWS TO KEEP OUT THE WIND-DREAMS

WILLIAM

> William told Rock he had done something incredible and that he had also heard a really good one. With his special-occasion talk, he had called one of the specialists at the General Hospital.
>
> They talked about Naomi and the famous laser operation! The hitch is, the rate of success is thirty not sixty per cent.

FRED-JAMES

> Ha! That's why at the grocery store old See-All asked me, in the dish detergent aisle, if Blackburn had finally convinced us to put Naomi away. Rock, that roach face Blackburn blows an ill wind on the Lastings.

WILLIAM

> Don't write anything on your paper, Rock, you might choke on the pencil.

LIGHTING THE THREE-THOUSAND-HOUR CANDLES

FRED-JAMES

Fred-James said to Rock: the holidays are coming. Like every year, the Lastings draw names for the exchange of presents. Fred-James said: I'll write everyone's name on a piece of paper.

Fred-James thought he was pretty clever 'cause he had put Rock and William's names in the hat twice. He had prepared a draw for reconciliation.

Go ahead, William! Oops, he said, it's my own name.

I shook the hat.

Try again! He pulled out a paper and read the name with a big smile.

Your turn, Rock. He draws and looks as happy as William.

My turn! I acted surprised when I drew a name, and one for Naomi.

I couldn't keep my mouth shut, I told William.

This morning, home from his errands, Rock, whose voice is back, says:

ROCK

I found the most beautiful present of all my draws, one helluva beautiful present. Hey, bozos, don't even try to find it!

FRED-JAMES
When Rock said that, William, all excited, felt joy in
his heart because he saw his brother rejoining the
Lasting Love Society.

Dark. Light. Say with the Say-Sayer.

WILLIAM
Naomi, every Christmas, you'd make us look at our
stretched faces in the tree ornaments; red faces,
blue, green, you said we came from another planet.

Dark. Light. Say soundlessly:

ROCK
Look, Naomi, I've cooked the Christmas turkey.

WILLIAM
Let's put a pretty tablecloth, makes everything taste
better.

FRED-JAMES
Oh! Look at the beautiful Christmas log!

WILLIAM
Tonight there's a feast at the Lastings'.

FRED-JAMES
I'll get the candles.

ROCK
What else!

WILLIAM
Some wine and brandy!

FRED-JAMES
Yahoo, wrapped-up presents!

Say with the sound of the voice:

WILLIAM

If the end of the world enters by the door to the north tonight, it'll catch us all merry!

Dark. Light.

ROCK

Look, Naomi, what's about to make an entrance? The deep cold of January.

FRED-JAMES

Four of us, in front of the TV, on the sofa-bed, not budging, blanketed up to our noses, looking at tapes of old shows.

WILLIAM

We took turns coming out from under the covers. A turn for food, a turn to change the tape, a turn to clean up Naomi, a turn for stoking the stove in the cellar, except for me, I never go down into the cellar now, can't take it. Puts me in a terrible state. I have so many nightmares where I'm in some cellar, even in broad daylight I let other people go down for me.

FRED-JAMES

Oh, no! Who blew that one! Get out of here!

WILLIAM

Yuk, Fred-James! Pig, you're gonna asphyxiate us.

FRED-JAMES

It's Naomi.

ROCK

Impossible! We just changed her.

WILLIAM

It's you, Rock. It smells of your farts.

ROCK
I'm telling you, it's not me.

WILLIAM
Don't you dare say: it's William.

ROCK
Light some matches, do something.

FRED-JAMES
~~Oops! It's Naomi, she's caught another stomach flu.~~

~~Dark. Light. Say into the Say-Sayer:~~

ROCK
Naomi, when you were little, ~~you used to play Queen of the Clock. Everywhere you went, you~~'d ~~tell people the time, because on the fridge, there was a golden clock set in a queen's carriage. Drawn by twelve horses, all gold too.~~
Look, I had it fixed for you, just for you.
Naomi's Carriage.

Dark. Light.

ROCK
~~We haven't even been to see the girls from the Capital!~~ Darn near unforgivable!

WILLIAM
Right!

FRED-JAMES
Before Naomi, we used to do all sorts of stuff.
What did we used to do?

ROCK
If the three of us died in one fell swoop, who'd take care of Ginginge?

Dark. Light. The Say-Sayer close by.

FRED-JAMES

Ginginge, look, a housefly in the middle of winter!
I heated her up for you. You hear that, it sounds
like summer.

Dark. Dark of night.

ROCK

Naomi is suffocating! Naomi! Turn on the lights,
Fred-James, quick!

FRED-JAMES

I can't find the switch.

WILLIAM

I strike a wooden match.

ROCK

Naomi, you alright? We're right here with you. She
seems to be lookin' at us. Can you see us, Naomi?

WILLIAM

Hello there! Sweet Ginginge!

ROCK

Your little brother, Fred-James!

FRED-JAMES

Do you recognize your brothers?

WILLIAM

She's laughing. She's laughing.
Sing, sing it to us, sweet Ginginge.

NAOMI

And.....

And.....

And.....

And.....

WILLIAM
Sing, Naomi, keep singing.

FRED-JAMES
Can you talk to us, Naomi?

ROCK
Shhh, let's not push her.

FRED-JAMES
I'm going to sleep here.

WILLIAM
Me too.

ROCK
Okay, we'll stay with her.

Dark. Light.

WILLIAM
Keeping watch over Naomi, day and night. Since March. Nothing, less than nothing. Not another sound.

Dark. Light.

ROCK
Look, Naomi, off in the distance, what do you see? It's Spring! Blow out what's left of the candles.

THREE BROTHERS
Once again, we made it through the winter.

WILLIAM
I open the "don't-open-till-spring" cedar-made closet for our lighter clothes.

ROCK
We're going out, Naomi, for a breath of air. Come into our six arms.

THE SAYING:

MOODY WAVES BREAK OVER THE HOUSE

WILLIAM

William said, with his new leader's voice, they
should get the summer set-up working again.
Come the first really hot days, we set Ginginge up
in her outdoors machine.
Brothers, I have something to say to you. I've
reasoned Naomi's sickness.
When she used to sing, people loved her like a star.
Other people, not just us, have to come to see her
and make her feel loved. She needs a mountain of
love to get better. A mountain of love!
I already talked to Madam See-All about it. She'd
be happy to help us. Tomorrow night, she could
come with the women from the 4H.
Unmad your eyes, Rock!

ROCK

Are you crazy? Naomi's not a firefly we can trap in a
jar and show off to just anyone.

WILLIAM

Rock, give me a few days.

ROCK

Do what you want, headslasher! You think just
because I was nice to you all winter I've forgotten
what you did to me?

FRED-JAMES

We got nothing to lose, Rock. I agree, I already told
him yes.

ROCK

Ha! I'm the last one to be consulted! You were
right, William, I guess we're not brothers anymore.

WILLIAM

Rock, don't bring that up again, I already told you,
I went too far. My brother, my brother ...

ROCK

Don't touch me! I'm never gonna speak to you
again.

FRED-JAMES

Rock closed himself in the bedroom, dead-bolted.
The next night, the 4H Ladies showed up with
their husbands and a slew of kids. Let's just say we
were surprised to see so many people.

WILLIAM

I asked you all to come here so you can say, one by
one, in our Say-Sayer, your happy memories and
other nice things to our sister, in the hope of her
great cure.

FRED-JAMES

"Is it true she lights up like the fountain in the
park? What time does she light up? Does she still
sing once in a while?" That's all they could say.

WILLIAM

I went knocking on Rock's door every hour.

Rock, my brother, open your door for me.

You should come see, people are being so generous
with our sister. They're talkin' about nice things,
even about love, like I asked them to.

FRED-JAMES

William sent me to tell you what's happenin'. Rock, are you there?

There are people standing around talking everywhere you look. Everyone takes a turn with the Say-Sayer. William tells them, thanks for comin', real polite, but they won't leave, they want to see Naomi light up.

Madam See-All must've blabbed too much.

WILLIAM

Rock, my brother, open the door for me.

It went really well. Now we're gonna tell them we have to close the yard.

FRED-JAMES

Almost all of them were in their cars when a little girl straggling behind yelled: "She's lighting up, she's lighting up." The news spread. An hour later, almost all the municipals were sitting in their lawnchairs, keeping watch, in case Naomi lit up again.

WILLIAM

Rock, my brother, open the door for me.

FRED-JAMES

William and me, we're gonna havta take turns, every four hours, watchin' over Naomi. We told them to leave, but they all want to stay. The lady municipals keep remindin' us of all their helping hands when we lost our parents. Like William says, it'd be a damn shame to send them away.

You wouldn't like it, Rock! Some of these people got no manners, they're doin' their business in the yard, in the garden, even.

They won't listen to reason. But they'd listen to you
if you told them to leave, for sure. Please come,
Rock.

WILLIAM

Rock, my brother, open your door for me.

Don't worry, I'll be right outside. I'm gonna sleep
in The Bull, close to Naomi, just in case.

ROCK

In the dark, I touch my face. Day by day, we don't
realize it, but when you think about it, there's
always some fear that haunts us constantly. And
fear, sad to say, is a hiding place for sorrow.

Sorrow is just a rude character who, if he hangs
round long enough, finally carves his name into
our clown faces.

WILLIAM

Rock, my brother, open your door for me.

We're hungry. You're such a good cook, and, me, I
can't fry an egg without breaking the yolk. Rock!

FRED-JAMES

Rock, things got outta hand, people are comin'
from other municipalities. I'm afraid we're gonna
lose control.

William thinks Naomi's gettin' better but I'm not
so sure. You should come take a look at her.

WILLIAM

Rock, my brother, open your door for me.

What should I do? People are throwin' coins in the
bathtub and makin' wishes. I told them: No, no
money, just come talk into the Say-Sayer, say sweet
loving things for our sister.

FRED-JAMES

Rock, Madam See-All's niece has shown up with the Regional Television. For a special report. They want to interview us.

WILLIAM

Excuse the mess! We don't usually have guests indoors. Guys livin' alone, you know how it is.

ROCK

William! Kick that bunch of snoops out of our house!

WILLIAM

Rock, my brother, open your door for me.

Forget about cooking, that's settled. We order from the restaurant and they deliver.

ROCK

If, for a moment, I stopped juggling in my head, if I didn't say another thing, if I stopped hearing and seeing, like before coming into this world, maybe then, deep in the silence of silence, inside my body, I could marry the Thunder's sister.

FRED-JAMES

Rock, I'm sittin' here with William. Come watch the report Madam See-All's niece did. It's starting, we can see you that time you made your public statement.

ROCK

Fred-James, go guard your sister immediately!

WILLIAM

Rock, what does unsanity mean? People said we live in unsanity conditions. Rock, answer me, do we live that way?

ROCK

I heard your loving friends say 'unsanitary.'
Un-san-i-ta-ry!

WILLIAM

Why won't they leave us alone? The mayor even
called us thunderstruck retards, right on TV! I'm
gonna punch his damn roachface in!

FRED-JAMES

William, you better come talk some sense into the
people who want to visit the house.

You broke the TV!

WILLIAM

That same night, when Fred-James and me were
outside, I saw Rock in the porthole-window in the
door to the north: I know you've come out of your
room and you're there watchin' us. Come help us,
my brother.

FRED-JAMES

In the middle of the night: William, wake up, it's
your turn to keep watch. What's that dirty little
smile on your face?

WILLIAM

'Cause of my dream, the girls from the Capital were
kissin' me, tearin' my clothes off to untease my
itch.

FRED-JAMES

Then, the following afternoon, guess who shows up
at our place: "Yoohoo! Yoohoo! Guys, it's Hortense
and Mimi. We've come to pay you a little visit. Is it
true about your sister? Is this really where you live?
Unbelievable!"

Did you ask them to come?

WILLIAM

A little whoopee-doo present for my brother Rock.

FRED-JAMES

Don't you realize this whole circus is embarrassin'
him to death. Send them away!

WILLIAM

Rock, the take-advantage people think that Naomi
can cure their booboos. They want their picture
taken beside the machine. You should see the yard,
it's a damn shame.

Rock, don't abandon us.

FRED-JAMES

Rock, please talk to William. Are you makin' him
suffer out of revenge? Tomorrow morning, you're
comin' out of there and you're gonna help us get
rid of everyone, you hear me? Now I'm fed up!

I'm afraid Naomi is dying.

WILLIAM

Catching us off guard, the unexpected showed up
on our doorstep again.

The Saying:

The Swamp Castle

THREE BROTHERS

Early in the morning, as they were watching dawn break, the Lasting brothers thought: the sun is real close. And everything came to an end-end on the first day of summer.

FRED-JAMES

William and me, we're burned with sun blisters, we're dying of a dangerous fatigue. We're a scary sight.

At nine o'clock, the wind rises. At ten o'clock, the yard is full of people again. Around eleven o'clock, the wind changes direction and arrives trailing black clouds.

WILLIAM

Rock, my brother, please open your door for me.

ROCK

You don't need a brother like me anymore.

WILLIAM

Open your door for me just one minute, you'll see my sad heart. You know we're brothers forever.

FRED-JAMES

The wind changes direction again, and again. Thunder claps in the distance. We start hearing the raindrops on the tin roof of the house.

WILLIAM

Gotta be kidding, tearin' a relic off our house!
Bunch of sickies! Get outta here! I'll give you a relic
on the jaw.

FRED-JAMES

Rock, Rock! William's gettin' beat up! Rock, they're
gonna kill him.

ROCK

What! Here I come, William my brother, here I
come!

FRED-JAMES

Just Rock's shouting is enough to scare those guys
away. That's when the mayor, our own, parks his
truck on the wrecked road, with his passenger, the
doctor Blackburn come to say: "the Lastings
machinations are over."

WILLIAM

The thunderclaps are coming closer, having a ball
banging the cardinal points together.

FRED-JAMES

Old Blackburn adds: "Right here, in my hand,
I've got a court order to take Naomi away; a
matter of public health. Your sister has to be
institutionalized."

WILLIAM

Never. Never. Body snatcher!

ROCK

Lousy roach face, scram! Why do you want to take
her away from us?

FRED-JAMES

Blackburn shouted to drown the thunder: "Your behaviour has become abnormal and illogical."

ROCK

The rain already has the force of a house on fire.

FRED-JAMES

A demented up-rooting. While we were arguing on the road, the municipals were crowding around Naomi's machine with scissors in their hands, they were cutting Naomi's hair down to her skull, they were even tearing her clothes to bits for relics.

My brothers, they're looting our sister.

THREE BROTHERS

At times like this, you have to say: "When sorrow to your home clings and cloys, mark the morrow for future joys."

ROCK

Lightning bolts are leading the way for chaos. Thunder is waiting there, at the end of our land, standing with both feet in the swamp. Our mouths have become like the skies about to release our anger.

Nobody will ever touch Ginger again.

FRED-JAMES

I bring out the rifles and the hunting knives, our own.

WILLIAM

Lightning bolts strike the ground. Rock and me, we beat with our fists to demolish the body snatchers around Ginginge's machine.

FRED-JAMES

Take the knives, our own. I'll load the guns.

WILLIAM

Get the hell outta here or I'll slit your throats.

FRED-JAMES

Madam See-All has arrived, holding her hat against the wind, with Blackburn, shouting to us: "Calm down, Lasting brothers, you're making things worse." I was keeping them at a distance with a loaded rifle.

Stay where you are.

ROCK

We run to cut the straps on Ginger's machine.

Don't cry, don't cry, brother William.

NAOMI

And....

WILLIAM

You crying too? We won't let them take our Lasting love sister away, eh, Rock?

ROCK

Never, William, never. They won't take our sister away from us.

Rock recognizes his own voice crying. He figures the time has come to take care of those tears.

FRED-JAMES

The municipals are invading our house. They are fighting over our clothes, our cups, our candles, our golden carriage with twelve horses and the door to the north, our own. Not even the mayor can control them.

My brothers, my brothers, they're stealin' our
house and home.

NAOMI

And....

WILLIAM

We don't know where to turn.

FRED-JAMES

Rock, they're gonna steal the Say-Sayer, our own.

NAOMI

And....

ROCK

Fred-James, you guard Ginger.

FRED-JAMES

With the rifle: Stay where you are!

ROCK

Flaming-burning-pointed-jagged lightning bolts are
ripping the sky apart.

WILLIAM

I run after the thief. Waving my arms in the air, I'm
holding a knife, my own. A lightning bolt rips down
my arm and forks to the left. A ball of fire bursts
out of my big toe. The red ball rolls over to the
stopped cars.

I keep running after the thief with the Say-Sayer; I
run-limp because of the burning. Then the balls of
fire shooting from my big toe catch the thief. I grab
the Say-Sayer, I've saved it.

ROCK

The storm is still shattering the sky, so bad chunks
of it are falling into the muddy yard.

FRED-JAMES

Stay where you are, Blackburn. I'm protecting Ginginge. A lightning-snake tears the rifle from my hands and beats his roach face with the butt. Great Thunder joins in and smashes a handful of house and home destroyers.

ROCK

Somebody pins me down with his gun on the hood of a car. Great Thunder, our brother-in-law, our own, descends on him, head first, the car explodes.

FRED-JAMES

Lightning strikes at the heart of the tree out front and it falls on the mayor's truck. The storm is on the Lastings' side.

WILLIAM

Another lightning bolt enters the Say-Sayer and bullets shower everyone and they run to hide in the ditch.

FRED-JAMES

A kind of up-rooting of life.

THREE BROTHERS

The rain pours down, our lashes are soaked, water enters through our mouths and spews back out with our wild cries.

There, we're alone.

ROCK

Fred-James, William, my dear brothers, they'll never get our Ginger. You hear the Thunder, he's come back to fetch his wife, Naomi.

Let's go, let's go to the end of the land, our own.

FRED-JAMES

We take Ginginge into our arms, our own six arms.
In the far distance, we can hear the police sirens.

THREE BROTHERS

The three of them are running and carrying their
sister. Naomi opens her eyes, the three brothers'
mouths tell her: "Don't be scared, the Lasting Love
Society is rewelded together."

They run all the way to the little woods at the end
of the land, their own, now a swamp.

FRED-JAMES

They hear the sirens of catastrophe. Hurry, we're
being chased.

ROCK

My brothers, can you hear me? We'll head for
Naomi's castle. She's prepared our rooms for us.
Tonight is our sister's big wedding, she's marrying
the Thunder.

WILLIAM

Husband Thunder is travelling at our side followed
by a loving party of eighty thousand lightning bolts
striding on their stilts.

ROCK

Run, run, the Lasting Love Society.

FRED-JAMES

Run, the Love Society, run.

WILLIAM

Holding their sister in their arms, they are still
running.

ROCK

They race through the little woods all the way to the edge of the swamp. The ground is wet, they are walking in water. Now the water is up to their knees. They press forward up to their waists.

Our sister, our own, is floating on the surface of the water, above the fieldstone castle. She's watching us carry her through the trees.

NAOMI

And....

FRED-JAMES

She's singing for us.

WILLIAM

The Lasting brothers slowly sink their sister into the water of the swamp.

ROCK

Rock said: may your hands hold your knives proudly.

Time to leave, William. Time to leave, Fred-James

WILLIAM

The Husband Thunder enters the swamp to lift his wife out of the water. With the Say-Sayer in her hands, she sings:

NAOMI

And....

And....

FRED-JAMES

Our sister is alive and great.

ROCK

Rock said: we are leaving, the Lasting Love Society, we are leaving.

WILLIAM

William and his two brothers see a door swing open. At last, at last!

FRED-JAMES

Fred-James shouts: At long last-last, the castle of light!

NAOMI

And….

And….

THREE BROTHERS

In the water of the swamp, the lightning bolts enter the Say-Sayer for the world to come.

For the world to come.

Abruptly, blinding flash of light.

THREE BROTHERS

Abruptly, they pierced their eardrums.

Abruptly, dark. Abruptly, light.

THREE BROTHERS

Abruptly, they gouged their eyes.

Abruptly, half-dark.

THREE BROTHERS

Abruptly, they cut off their tongues.

Gently, dark.